The Bible Fact or Fiction?

By Earl Robinson

ISBN 0-88019-296-8

Schmul Publishing Co., Inc.
Wesleyan Book Club   1992   Salem, Ohio

Printed by
Old Paths Tract Society
Shoals, IN 47581

Table of Contents

CHAPTER	PAGE
Introduction	5
1. Does a Supreme Being Exist?	9
2. Prophecy and Inspiration	20
City of Tyre in Prophecy	21
Babylon in Prophecy	22
The Jews in Prophecy	25
Jesus in Prophecy	29
3. Scientific Evidence in Inspiration	31
Proof from Medicine	32
Proof from Physical Science	33
4. The Bible Speaks for Itself	37
5. The Testimony of Experience	43
6. Evidence of the Virgin Birth	48
7. Why Men Disbelieve the Gospel	59

Introduction

As far as is known, more Bibles are published today then any other single book. However, this was not always so. There was a time in Europe that it was a violation of the law, in certain places, to have a Bible in your possession. And even now as well as in past years, the claim of the book to be a message from God has, and is being denied. Those who question the Bible as being an inspired book are known as doubters, agnostics, and atheists. A doubter can be defined as one who is uncertain and unsettled with regard to its authority; an atheist is one who says flatly there is no God; and an agnostic is one who says if there is a God, it is impossible to know it. Any reliable evidence of the truth of inspiration will, then, depend on two things: First, is there a supreme Being. Second, if so has He in any way communicated with people on this planet. Before answering these questions, let us first notice just that parts of the Bible are specifically denied. First, inspiration of the Bible as an enlightenment by the Holy Spirit. Second, the personality of the Holy Spirit. Third, the virgin birth, miracles, divinity and sinlessness of Jesus. Fourth, the Genesis story of creation.

These among others are some of the fundamental teachings of the Bible that are being denied. And this denial has come not only from non-Christians but also from those who are pastors of churches. Among those who insist that the Bible is not the Book it claims to be are such men as Robert Ingersoll, an infidel and American orator, Tom Paine, author of "Age of Reason," Earnest Renan, an English religious historian, Dr. Nils Terre, author, lecturer and notorious infidel, and Harry Fordick, a noted American minister.

Since the inspiration of the Bible is the all important issue, just what is meant by inspiration?

The inspiration of the Bible is a topic that has been discussed throughout the ages. Its importance lies in the fact that if the Bible is merely a man-made book, it becomes subject to mistakes and errors. However, if God Himself is behind the Book, then with confidence we can accept its principles, history, and scientific statements as true. If, however, God had nothing to do with this book in any special way, then its accuracy and authority can certainly be questioned. Also, it should be noted that throughout the manuscript, the Bible is quoted as evidence. It, then, is imperative that its authority be established on evidence which a reasonable mind cannot reject. Then, too, this topic will be discussed with reference to Rev. Weatherhead's book, *The Christian Agnostic.*

Notice first that a word is of little or no value unless its meaning is known. With reference to the word inspiration, Webster defines it as a "Divine influence on the mind." That the writers of the Bible were influenced in some manner by the Living Spirit of God has been accepted as true throughout the ages. However, in more recent time not only has "this Divine influence" on the mind been by some rejected, there seems to be no general agreement between Christians as to the *how* of inspiration. On this point three theories will be discussed.

1. The first is known as the dictation theory. This means simply that every word in the Bible was in some way dictated by the Holy Spirit. The writer held the pen and wrote the words that flowed into his mind. This method is not unlike that of a stenographer who records the words spoken by another.

2. The second is known as the illumination theory. According to this theory, a general illumination or enlightenment by the Spirit of the writer's mind was made. Ideas, facts, or principles were revealed. However, the exact words by which these ideas, principles, or facts were expressed depended upon each individual writer. What they otherwise could not have known was revealed to them. Then each author selected the words by which the fact, principle, idea, truth, or event was expressed.

3. A combination of the two above theories is the third. Notice that thoughts and words are the two sides of the same coin. For a coin to exist with only one side is impossible. And as far as is known, to think without words is also impossible. The Spirit, then, could not reveal a fact or a coming event without using words. Therefore, He must have dictated the words used by the writer. However, this did not exclude the possibility of each writer in giving the substance of the message in his own words. Whether this actually occurred, we have no way of knowing.

These are, then, three ways by which the Spirit could have illuminated or dictated the Bible to those who wrote this marvelous book. And although some may have stumbled over the way by which God revealed or gave His message to men, the question to remember is this: Is the Bible in any way an inspired book? That question we will attempt to answer.

CHAPTER ONE

Does A Supreme Being Exist?

With reference to any discussion of the reliability of the Bible the question concerning a Supreme Intelligence cannot be ignored. If the universe always existed, and no personal intelligence, energy, or power brought it into being, then, the Bible cannot be a message from Him. Men endowed with great powers of intellect have taken an honest look at the moral condition of men, of suffering, pain, and death and declared how can these things be if a Being of Supreme goodness and power is in existence. The individual communists rejects the concept of God's existence; the atheists also declare there is no God. The agnostics affirm if God exists it is impossible to know Him; and perhaps there has flashed across the minds of the majority of men at some time in their life, the disquieting doubt that perhaps, after all, there is no God.

Consider, then, the results and conditions of things if there were no Supreme Power. If the contentions of the atheists are true, all hopes of a future life, with all that involves, dissolves before the grave. The uncounted evils that one person has suffered at the hands of another will never be rectified. That justice, then, will finally triumph over wrong is merely wishful thinking with no basis in fact. Without God, moral laws, do not exist. Each of us is a law unto himself. To steal and murder are not evils in themselves but simply the natural expressions of one's nature. If there is no God, the great principle of self denial about which Jesus taught, and of which He is the greatest Example, is so much nonsense. Without God all explanations of the universe, including life, are mere speculations. Without God the dark traits of character, such as hostility, revenge, greed and hate, can never be eradicated from the soul. Real peace, then, as a result of divine forgiveness is not possible. Without a Supreme Intelligence, therefore, all hopes, longings, aspirations and a dawning sense of incompleteness apart from God, are all buried without remedy in the grave.

Do those, then, who reject the idea of a Supreme Being believe in anything? They do, for a man to live without some kind of faith is impossible. Here is the faith of the atheist as given by G. H. Hardy in his little book *Countdown,* page 13.

1. No supernatural power exists.
2. All creation is the product of chance or as some believe, the physical universe always existed.
3. Living matter comes from death matter.
4. Intelligence and conscience appeared without sponsorship.

Now notice—if these four statements are true, then there is no need for a God. This is what the disbeliever is telling us. All creation is the result of chance, for things always existed. Why should he insist that God exists when such a being is not called for? And so long as man possesses intelligence, the sun shines, and the rain falls, man can live and direct his own affairs without the assistance from a supernatural source. It is clear at once that if there is no God, then the Bible cannot be a message from Him. However, the earth and the entire universe must be accounted for. It was either created or it always existed. According to the four above statements, the physical universe always existed. And all living things originated from dead inorganic matter. The name given to that theory or process to account for all life is called evolution. Those who do not accept the Bible as a message from God to man, accept the evolutionary idea to account for the physical universe and all types of life upon it. Before, then, giving the evidence that there is indeed a Being known as God, we will first discuss the subject of evolution.

1. The whole idea of evolution is only a theory or a guess. It has never been proven true, and indeed cannot be. Sir Arthur

Keith said: "Evolution is unproved and unprovable. We believe it because the only alternative is special creation, and that is unthinkable." When speakers or writers of articles of books refer to evolution as a proven fact, if done intentionally, they are simply telling a falsehood.

2. All the evidence of the truth of evolution such as mutation, paleontology, embryology, comparative anatomy and domestication—all contains flaws which makes it impossible to arrive at conclusions beyond question. Paleontology, for example, is a study of fossils through geological periods. In interpreting the fossil records, scientists have often been wrong and downright frauds have, at times, been perpetrated. An example was the piltdown man which scientists did not discover to be a fraud for forty years.

Another point of great importance connected with fossils is this: No fossil ever found has proven to be a missing link between a higher and a lower organism. This statement flatly contradicts the one made by W. F. Pauli, author of a biology textbook, *The World of Life*. He states, on page 103, that a fossil of a bird found in Bavaria is a "missing link." Now notice two facts about fossils as connecting links between lower and higher forms of life. First, fossilized skeletons when found have always been that of a fully developed animal or plant. That is, no part of the skeleton shows evidence of evolving into some other form. Second, if evolution is true, there ought to be not one missing link but thousands if not millions of them in all stages of development. Yet no one single fossil has ever been found that could remotely connect the highest order of apes to man. More on this point in the next paragraph.

3. The most telling point for the theory is the similarity that basically exists between all living things. This is a scientific fact. However, this similarity has to do with the physical structure of plants and animals. When the life of the plant or animal is considered the story is different. If all life had its origin in a single cell, then that life must continue in an unbro-

ken line to man himself. From the fossil record, there is no way this can be proven. Going back now to Pauli's so-called missing link, that fossil was simply another species of birds which, like other species, became extinct. Nowhere on earth today does such a bird exist. And the peculiar kind of life that produced such a bird died with it.

One more illustration of the flaws in the evidence for evolution is mutation. The author above already referred to, Wolfgang F. Pauli, said on page 106, that mutations are one of the strongest arguments for the theory of evolution. Yet natural selection and mutation (which are said to be the mechanism of evolution) certainly do not fit very well together. Natural selection means simply that nature selects the individual plant or animal that is to survive. Mutation is the sudden appearance of a characteristic in a plant or animal not possessed by the species. Now notice—the purpose of natural selection is to eliminate the unfit. A mutation may occur in any plant or animal—fit or unfit. Nature, then, works at cross-purposes with herself. Mutations do occur. Natural selection is only a theory—a guess as to how evolution, if true, carries on her work.

4. Evolutionists really are not sure about anything. This uncertainty is revealed in their writings by the use of such words as probably, it is believed, it is thought, or it could have been this way. Every piece of the puzzle which evolutionists say is evidence will, upon close scrutiny, reveal obstructions which destroys that piece as evidence. The whole idea that man, therefore, evolved from lower forms of life, is from start to finish, based upon assumptions, and pure guess work. "Federal Judge, Whilfield Davison said on this point: Under the rules of circumstantial evidence, the evolutionist could not establish any fact before a judge and jury."

Now compare the faltering doubtful tone of the evolutionist with the bold emphatic declaration of Moses, "In the beginning God created—and God, in the sea created every living creature—after their kind. And every winged fowl, in the air, after his kind, And on the land, God made the beasts of the earth after his kind—" Genesis 1st chapter.

5. In spite of the fact that the words, "after his kind," refer to the completed act, the strongest evidence against evolution are those very words. The bird-life can only produce another bird; the fish-life another fish; and human-life another human. Since all life is not the same kind of life, when one kind of life ceases to be that plant or animal becomes extinct. Life is the organizing principle of every living thing. The life of the apple tree from its environment organizes that kind of a plant. It is impossible for it to bring forth any other kind of plant but the apple tree. And the same principle holds for every living thing since life can only produce life after its kind, Provisions, it should be noted, have been made for variations or change within groups or species. Mutants and hybrids are evidence of this change. However, a limit has been set even here. The species is a fixed unbreakable unit. To my knowledge, the evolutionist cannot cite one single example a million years ago or now of where the species of one animal or plant has ever been crossed with another. Here is an obstruction in the path of the evolutionist that makes of this theory the lie of the ages.

The evolutionist accounts for all living things by assuming that life had its beginning from a single speck of living matter. This living speck or cell originated in some slimy sea millions of years ago. If this speck of matter was *living* then its life came spontaneously. Yet scientists have proven that there is no such thing as spontaneous generation of life. Therefore, this one fact is another broken link in the chain of evidence for the evolutionary hypothesis. And this fact also brands the whole idea that the complex forms of life developed from simpler forms as false, untenable, and one of the most fantastic lies ever fostered upon the intellect of man.

The other alternative to account for life on this planet is that all life came from pre-existing life. And notice, too, that each type of life must have come from its own kind. This we know is true not only from our own observations now but also from the study of fossils. Every skeleton, as related above, of a fossil has been that of a plant or animal which could be recognized and classified. That is if the fossil, for example, was that of a young ape, there were no indications from the skeleton of it developing or growing into some higher form of life like man. There is no other life on earth, for example, like that of the ape. It is a fixed unchangeable quality, or unit. There is no provision in this kind of life for it to grow or develop into anything else or animal but another ape. If this year all apes on earth were to become extinct, there is no other life on earth that can produce or develop another ape. And this holds true for all forms of life on earth. This, then, is the situation now and judging from fossils' forms, this was true of all past ages since life first appeared on this planet.

Due, then, to the fact that all life is not the same kind of life, every class, species, or variety of plants or animals must bring forth another plant or animal like itself. Since, therefore, all life must or has come from pre-existing life, define it as you may, it must have been created. And if created, there must have been or is a creator—God.

Leaving the evolutionist with his unproven theory, here is what David said on the creation of man: "My substance was not hid from thee, when I was in secret, curiously wrought in the lowest part of the earth. Thine eyes did see my substance, yet being unperfect; and in thy book all members were written, which in continuance were fashioned, when as yet there was none of them" Psalm 139:15-16. Evolution, therefore, cannot account for the solar system nor for plant and animal life on the earth. Since all things had a beginning, we are forced to the conclusion that a Supreme Intelligence is in existence. However, faith without evidence is really not faith. It is credulity what is is the evidence that there is an all-knowing, all-powerful Being in existence? The first line of evidence has to do with design. This word has, at least, seven different meanings. To set apart for some purpose, is the sense the word *design* will be used here. This planet, then, bears evidence of having been planned or designed for some purpose. The argument is that if the earth was designed for some purpose, it obviously had a Designer. What, then is the evidence that this earth was planned by some great Intelligence, and what was His purpose?

Assume some celestial being should come to this planet. He possessed no previous knowledge of the earth nor of the life that exists upon it. Now a living thing must have Life within itself, or it must depend for its existence upon an environment. This celestial being, then, would soon discover that while life resides in the organism, yet for its continued existence, each living thing, without an exception, obtains its nourishment from its own environment. This celestial being would also discover that certain general principles must be "just right" if the correct relationship is to exist between the organism and its environment. Notice the following examples of how precise must be the conditions of the environment as it is related to life.

1. Our atmosphere is prevented from flying into space because of the gravity pull upon it. Its height is exactly right, then, for the sustenance of life. This could not be the case if the earth was not exactly the correct size.
2. The mixture of gases in the atmosphere had to be in the correct proportion for the following results to occur:
   a. The breathing apparatus of living things is exactly suited to this mixture.
   b. The atmosphere prevents the earth from scorching by day and freezing by night.
   c. The rays from space that could destroy all life are filtered out by the gas ozone.
3. The school boy knows that the earth tilts 23.5 degrees from the perpendicular. A tilt less or greater would produce flood, extreme heat and frigid cold.

4. The speed of the earth around the sun and its rotation is another feature that must be exactly correct if life as we know it is to exist. As a matter of common knowledge, Mercury is a planet with a temperature of 770 degrees on one side, and almost absolute zero on the other. As an example of a planet where conditions were not right, Mercury on one side is always dark and cold, and the other hot and light.
5. Another one of those things which had to be nearly perfect if life on earth was to exist is the distance of the earth from the sun. From this glowing ball of fire, heat, light, and power is obtained. If the sun was a few degrees closer, living things would die from an excessive amount of heat. If a few degrees farther away, the earth would become a huge ball of ice floating in space.

These examples are a few among many revealing how exact must be the conditions of the environment in its relation to living things. If these conditions—the size of the earth, the mixture of gases, the tilt of the earth, the speed of rotation, and the distance of the earth from the sun—were altered to any perceivable degree, living things sooner or later would disappear from the earth.

Now the atheist tells us that these exacting conditions are the result of blind chance. The earth just happened to be the correct size, the right distance from the sun, and exactly the right speed. There was no intelligence involved in the mixture of the gases of our atmosphere. It just happened that way. Take your choice. As for me, in view, then, of these five conditions and to life, can there exist a reasonable doubt that a great Intelligence designed the earth for the habitation of living things?

There is another fact which our visitor from outer space would soon discover. And that is the marvel of how living things are adapted to their environment. When an animal fits into its environment it is said to be adapted to that environment. Of this adaptation a hundred examples could be given. "In all organisms, then, there is an inherited fitness for a particular kind of habitat. This fact, in general, explains why animals live where they do." Animals, then, live in the water, the land, in the ground, and in the air because they are mentally and physically made to fit in these environments. As a matter of common knowledge, the bird equipped with wings can move through the air; animals of every kind and description equipped with lungs can fit into a land environment; and a fish equipped with gills is adapted to live in the water.

This adaptation of a bird to the air, of a man to land, or a fish to the water came about in one of three ways—by chance, by a developing process called evolution, or by the exercise of an intelligent process called creation.

That blind chance could account for one or two of these conditions is possible. Yet when many such conditions upon which life depends are involved, chance is ruled out. And the fact is that first germ of life could have come only from pre-existent life.

Third, on the question of God's existence, given below are four statements from the book, *Man Does Not Stand Alone* by A. C. Morrison, a former president of the Academy of Science. They are given with little or no comment.

1. "The resourcefulness of life to accomplish its purpose is a manifestation of an all-pervading intelligence. Life is a sculptor, a musician, and a sublense chemist—Behold an almost invisible drop of protoplasm, transparent, jelly-like—. This single cell holds within itself the germ of life—nature did not create life; fire-blistered rocks and saltless sea could not meet the necessary requirements. Who, then, put it there?
2. Provisions for all living is revealed in such phenomena as the wonders of genes. Here, evolution really begins—at the cell, the entity which holds and carries the genes. That the ultramicroscopic

gene can absolutely rule all life on earth is an example of profound cunning—that could emanate only from a creative intelligence; no other hypothesis will serve.
3. By the economy of nature, we are forced to realize that only infinite wisdom could have foreseen and prepared with such astute husbandry.—Such checks and balances have been universally provided. Unless these physical checks had been provided man could not exist. Imagine meeting a hornet as big as a lion.
4. The fact that man can conceive the idea of God is in itself a unique proof.

In connection with this subject, notice another idea. It has been said that in reality no normal person disbelieves in the existence of a Supreme Being. The evidence against the idea and the inherent desire of men to worship something is too overwhelming. Rather what is denied is a lack of contact or correspondence with a spiritual world. Henry Drummond has this to say on this point, "But this is just what they tell us they have not. What they deny is not God. It is the correspondence. The very confession of the unknowable is in itself the dull recognition of an environment beyond themselves. And for which they felt they lack the correspondence."

Professor Drummond, in the above words, has expressed the crucial point with reference to this whole idea of God's existence. It is not, then, the existence of God so much that is denied. Rather it is the lack of contact with Him. Go where you please among men, and this lack of a saving relationship with a God of matchless love and grace is apparent. However, since the facts of His existence, in the light of reason, are difficult to deny, it is really the lack of communion with Him that is being questioned. What the communist, the atheists, the agnostics, and all doubters are really saying is that if there is a God, we do not know Him. There is not found in all nature a situation more pathetic than to behold men with the need and capacity to commune with Christ of the Spiritual World yet, due to a moral catastrophe, they cannot because they will not. And the tragedy is all the more pathetic, when it is remembered that in such a world is found the energy or power to meet every moral need.

There is, then, a God—a Supreme Being of infinite wisdom and unlimited power. Every flower that blooms, every leaf that flutters in the breeze, the amazing complexity of the brain of animals and man, an environment to which all living things are perfectly adapted and the impossibility of life developing from dead inorganic matter—all these and more proclaim the existence of a God of love, mercy and justice beyond our comprehension.

CHAPTER TWO
Inspiration and Prophecy

The word prophecy has different yet similar meanings. It can mean any prediction of the future. Or it can mean any prediction of the future under the influence of divine guidance. In this chapter, the word will be used to mean the telling of the future by prophets who obtained their knowledge or information from God.

There are two aspects of prophecy which will be considered. One has to do with details. Suppose you are told that in fifty years the city of New York will be destroyed. This is a general statement and it could happen. However, it is of little or no value as evidence. Suppose I add details. The destruction will occur in the last month of the year 2050; the agency of destruction will be a tidal wave; every person within the city limits will die; and the city will never be rebuilt. Assuming that the city was destroyed exactly as foretold, the event now becomes indisputable prophetic evidence.

The time element in prophecy must also be considered. The greater the time between the foretelling of an event and its fulfillment increases the value of that prophecy as evidence. If 500 years, for example, elapse between the telling and the fulfillment of an event it would be more credible than if only fifty years had gone by. This is not to say that a prophecy which was fulfilled in fifty years is not reliable. Other factors, such as details, may be involved which would make it perfectly reliable prophetic evidence. As prophetic evidence is considered in support of the inspiration of the Bible, keep in mind these two factors—the time element and details in prophecy.

It is rather strange that Rev. Weatherhead makes no mention of prophecy in his chapter on the Bible and inspiration.

Yet G. D. Hardy in his book, *Countdown,* says that prophecy is the fingerprint of God. A fingerprint, you know, is an infallible method of identification. Only in the mind of God is the knowledge of an event hundreds of years before it occurs. Now, if a Biblical writer told in detail that a certain event would occur say 500 years before it happened, he could have received such knowledge only from One who possessed that knowledge. In fact, the prophet would be recording historical events which were yet to come. If, then, it can be proven that one man has from God received a single message, it follows that a way exists for communication between God and man.

Let us now consider some examples of events foretold by ancient prophets who lived in the dim distant past. And remember as you read these prophecies, you are looking backward some hundreds if not thousands of years. And the people, land, or city about which the prophecies are made seem so firm, and enduring, at the time, that those who read them when they were written, could only sneer in disbelief for they could not understand.

City of Tyre in Prophecy

This ancient city was located on the central eastern coast of the Mediterranean Sea. "The prophecy concerning the city is most intriguing. Prior to the event by 250 years, God, through Ezekiel foretold the destruction of Tyre by Alexander the Great, describing how the city would be leveled flat and its stones and timbers cast into the sea. And Alexander did just that, using everything in the city, scraping out its very earth to build a causeway to defeat the Phoenecians. It said that Tyre will never be rebuilt, and for 2500 years that prophecy has stood true. Not too surprising you say. Yet it's nothing short of amazing when you realize the Raselain's Springs are still here and could support a modern city." Observe now the details of this prophecy:

1. The city would be destroyed by an invading army.

2. Its stones and timbers would be cast into the sea. These came from the old city built on the coast of the sea.
3. The earth would be scraped leaving bare the rocks.
4. And the most amazing detail is this: The city would never be rebuilt.

To verify these details, one has but to turn to a book of ancient history that describes the destruction of this city. Notice also the time element. From the day Ezekiel wrote this prophecy to the day of its fulfillment, two hundred and fifty years went by.

If it can be shown that a prophecy fails of fulfillment in one single detail, that fact alone is sufficient to destroy the prophecy as evidence of inspiration. Here, then, is a way for those who say there is no God, nor of course, no message from Him; to disprove the truth of prophecy. And that is to rebuild the ancient city of Tyre. Russia, the greatest of the communist nations, has the resources to do just that. Since a hard-core, dyed-in-the wool communist denies the existence of God, the inspiration of the Bible, and in reality all moral principles, he has but to rebuild Tyre on the site where it was destroyed to disprove what Ezekiel foretold.

Babylon in Prophecy

This city was located in the upper valley of the Tigris and Euphrates Rivers. Nabopolassar was the founder of what is known as the Chaldean or Babylonian Empire (625-605 B.C.). This great city was the capital of this empire which arose to its greatest splendor under the renowned ruler, Nebuchadnezzar.

The prophecies with reference to this city assume a new significance if the size of the city is known. According, then, to ancient historians such as Herodotus and to the discoveries of archaeology, we have a fair idea as the physical size of the ancient city. In keeping with other great cities, Babylon was surrounded not by one, but two walls. These walls enclosed an immense area some 60 miles in circumference. By this is not meant that buildings occupied this whole area. Rather, these walls enclosed many acres of fertile land on which crops were grown. In the event of a siege, this arrangement would enable the inhabitants to grow food within its walls. As a means of greater protection from an encircling foe, a moat filled with running water surrounded the walls.

The walls were massive both in height and thickness. The outer wall was twenty-one feet thick, and the inner eleven. One account states that the walls were fifty feet thick, In height they stood 200 cubic inches which was equivalent to 300 feet. Beside these walls two others were built along both banks of the Euphrates River. This was due to the fact that the city was built on both sides of the river. And the river itself entered beneath the wall on one side and flowed out beneath the wall on the other side.

The fortifications of the city were, therefore, almost impregnable from an invading foe. The people, due to its walls, food supply, and an abundance of water had but little to fear, Such was the strength and size of the city when Isaiah and Jeremiah made their predictions concerning it.

For some 1500 years, this great city dominated the Tigris and Euphrates valley. Then in the year 538 B.C., a great Persian army led by Cyrus who himself was a man of prophecy, stood before the gates of the city. After defeating the Chaldeans in the open field, the gates to the city were opened to him. And without opposition he entered the city in the year 538 B.C.

The two great prophets who pronounced judgment against Babylon were Isaiah and Jeremiah. Details and the time element meet the requirements of evidential prophecy in their predictions. First, observe the details of these prophecies.

1. Babylon was to be captured by the people from the north. The direction mentioned is most intriguing. There were other directions from which an invading army could have come. Yet it was the Persians, an Aryan nation from the north and east, who took the city as Jeremiah predicted. Jer. 50:9.

2. One of the most remarkable details of prophecy concerning Babylon is the fact that it would never be rebuilt. The exact words of both Isaiah and Jeremiah are to the effect that the city would never be inhabited. This is nothing short of amazing when one remembers that ancient cities were often built on the site of an older city that had been destroyed, but whose foundation may still be intact. For Babylon to have attained its greatness both in area and population implies the site chosen was an excellent one. Yet the words of the prophets have stood true against the passing of time for some 2500 years. Jer. 50:39. Isaiah 13:20.

3. The future inhabitants of the ruins of Babylon were to be wild beasts of the desert. Dolefully howling creatures such as wild goats and jackals would dwell there. Contrast a scene, such as this, with those days when Babylon was a flourishing prosperous city whose fortifications were so formidable as to inspire awe and despair in the heart of a would-be conqueror. Now both prophets speak, while the city was still at the height of its glory, of coming desolation so profound as to arouse horror and astonishment in the minds of those who behold its ruins. Isaiah 13:30-51:48.

4. Looking into the future, the prophets named those who would shun the ruins of Babylon. No Arab would pitch his tent there; no shepherd would make his sheepfold there. In these words, it appears that the prophet is issuing a challenge to those who doubt the truth of their predictions. If, then, these words are not a true prophecy, how simple it would be to put them to a test. To prove that Isaiah was wrong, the Arabians have but to pitch their tents on the site of Babylon, and the shepherd to build there an enclosure for his sheep. On the contrary, the Arab will not, due to superstition, pitch his sheepfold there. Travelers who have visited the ruins of Babylon say that these words are literally true. The Arabians do shun this area and the sheep herder will not remain long in this forbidden and desolate area.

5. Isaiah (14:23) said that the site of Babylon would become "marshes and pools of water." This, too, is a remarkable prophecy in view of the fact that "Babylon was located in the midst of a very fertile area, and it would have seemed reasonable to suppose that, regardless of what happened to the population, the region would always furnish pasturage for flocks. But Isaiah said, to repeat, that it would become possession of wild animals, and be covered with marshes of water." After Babylon was taken the whole area around the city was covered by water due to the neglect of dykes and canals of the Euphrates River. It became stagnant marshes of water among ruins haunted by wild animals, and proclaiming to all who might see it, that surely as the Lord purposed, so shall it come to pass."

To enumerate more details of which there are many would be useless as far as establishing the truth of this prophecy. Remember, we are looking backward in time and therefore we have no difficulty in comparing these details with their actual fulfillment. From our vantage point, then, we can see the historical events which corroborate the words of the prophets.

Now notice the time element. "This whole prophecy is generally conceded to have been written long over a century (170) years before the downfall of Babylon. And this at a time when the circumstances for its fulfillment seemed most improbable. However, these prophecies state that Babylon, apparently secure within her massive walls, could be wiped from the face of the earth. Therefore, since no sagacity of the human mind could have foreseen the utter destruction of Babylon, the prophets could have obtained their knowledge only from one who knew God, and revealed knowledge from God."

The Jews and Prophecy

A look at the history of the Jews is most interesting. No people have endured the constant suffering and persecution as have the Jews and yet lived. And no people except the Jews can trace their descendants in an unbroken line back into the dim past of ancient times. Few marry outside their own people. And where on earth today are the direct descendants of the ancient Romans, the Chaldeans, the Babylonians, the Egyptians and the Persians? Not a single direct descendant of these ancient people can be found today among the inhabitants of this planet.

Below is given a list of the prophecies concerning the Jews. And remember they were spoken hundreds of years before the event occurred. Therefore, the prophets wrote in part the history of the Jews as if that history had already came to pass. Here, then, is a partial list of the prophecies concerning the Jews.

1. And thou shall become an astonishment, a proverb, and a byword, among all nations whither the Lord shall lead thee" Deuteronomy 28:37.
2. "Yet I will leave a remnant, that ye may have some that shall escape the sword among the nations, when ye shall be scattered through the countries" Ezekiel 6:3. Also the Jews were to be scattered among all nations—Jer. 24:9.
3. The Jews would be allowed to return to their homeland never again to be scattered among the nations. Isaiah 11:11-12, Amos 9:15.

Let us now briefly compare these prophecies with the known history of the Jewish people. First, they would remain a separate and distinct people. This is known from the fact that the Jews are the only ancient people who can trace their decent in an unbroken line back to Abraham. This is a remarkable fact of prophecy.

Second, they would be scattered among all nations. This prophecy has been fulfilled before the eyes of this generation. It was spoken by Moses some two thousand years ago. From the cold regions of the north to the equatorial regions of the south, and in all countries some Jews could be found. Scattered to the four winds of heaven, when Jerusalem fell to the Romans in 70 A.D., they settled in large numbers in cities throughout the world.

3. "Thou shall be an astonishment, a proverb, a byword among the nations." How literally, though spoken thousands of years ago, have these words been fulfilled. That their name has been used as a byword is common knowledge. And the fact that the Jew has amazed and astonished every one acquainted with their history is due to two reasons: The first has to do with their durability as a people. A fact, difficult in some respects to explain, is a strange hostility which sooner or later develops toward the Jew. This antagonism comes to the surface during a political or economic condition in which the Jews are involved. Then followed persecution in various ways often instigated by the government under which they lived. Living in one country, they might be forced, in large numbers, to migrate to another. Then their property was confiscated, or they might be killed by the thousands. Their suffering and deliberate murder by orders of Hitler was merely a repetition, on a large scale, of the persecution endured by them throughout the centuries. Yet no amount of distress, sufferings, and various kinds of persecutions have destroyed the Jews as a distinct people. This remarkable fact cannot be said about any other known nationality. And this fact is exactly what was predicted concerning them.

The second fact that has astonished those who are familiar with their history is their uncanny ability to amass wealth. A gifted person or people may acquire wealth without the world condemning him for it. However, with reference to the Jews, the fact is that his talent to acquire wealth often works against him. When he settles in a community, his business acumen soon enables him to acquire wealth. He may take over business establishments which in turn may arouse the enmity and envy of his neighbors. Persecution in different forms now follows, often including torture and death. Therefore, their ability to survive in the face of such conditions, and their talents to accumulate wealth has astonished those who know the history of these persecuted people. Over and over, this has been the pattern which has followed the Jewish people. And reading their history in the future, the prophets of old foretold their suffering, persecution, and death.

Observe one more event foretold more than a thousand years ago that is now in the process of being fulfilled. Here it is as found in Isaiah chapter 11, Jeremiah 33, Ezekiel 11; and Amos chapter 9:15, "And it shall come to pass that the Lord shall set his hand the second time to recover the remnant of his people—and shall assemble the outcast of Israel and gather the dispersed of Judah from the four corners of the earth—I will gather you from people, and assemble you out of the countries where ye have been scattered, and I will plant them upon the land, and they shall no more be pulled up out of the land which I have given them saith the Lord."—Concerning the prophecy notice five things:

1. 587 B.C. is the approximate time of this prophecy. Or counting from the 1969, the time is 2556 years ago.
2. From all countries in which they had been scattered, the Jews were to be re-established on their own land. (Palestine)
3. On May 14, 1948, Palestine under the Jews became a republic. Therefore, this prophecy is in the process of being fulfilled since individual Jews are still settling in the country.
4. Never again would the Jews be driven from their land.
5. The prophets who spoke these words declared emphatically that God had revealed to them this event.

This first part of the above prophecy has actually come to pass in our own day. To deny this is folly since more than 2,000,000 Jews have returned and now are living in Palestine. "Every laborious acre the Jews reclaim from the desert, every orange bud that blooms is triumph of the foreknowledge of God."

Notice, too, the Jews would never again be scattered among the nations. In trying, then, to drive the Israelites into the sea, the Arabians are beating their heads against the impregnable rock of prophecy.

Think, then, earnestly and soberly upon the prophetic history of the Jews. That history is a fact. And no honest man no matter if he be an intellectual genius can deny it. And this history beyond question is a part of the prophetic evidence of the truth of inspiration.

Jesus and Prophecy

Those prophecies concerning the Jews and the destruction of two ancient cities have been discussed. Turn now to another set of prophecies, those concerning Jesus Christ. That Jesus is or was a historical figure, that He actually walked the hills and valleys of Palestine is as well substantiated as any fact in history. These prophecies, also, go back for hundreds of years into the dim days of ancient times before Jesus appeared on earth.

Below are prophecies concerning the life of Jesus. They are:

1. Isaiah 7:14. Jesus would be born of a virgin. This prophecy was fulfilled in Luke 1:31.
2. Isaiah 50:6. Jesus would be spit on. The record of this fulfillment is found in Matt. 27:30 and Mark 15:19.
3. Micah 5:2. Jesus would be born in Bethlehem of Judaea. This fulfillment is recorded in Matthew 2:1 and Luke 2:4.
4. Zechariah 11:12. Jesus' betrayal for 30 pieces of silver. This event is recorded in Matthew 26:15.
5. Psalm 22:13. Fulfilled in Mark 15:24.

The facts which render these prophecies so important as evidence of inspiration are both the time and details. With reference to the time, they were spoken some 700 years before they came to pass. There was no possible way for the prophets to have known that these events would come to pass without being told. Notice some remarkable things about them. For example, Bethlehem, the town in which Jesus was born, did not even exist when this prophecy was spoken. Yet Micah named the town which, 700 years later, would be the birthplace of Jesus. Also, to predict the death of a man is not a remarkable thing to do, since all men must die. However, to tell the manner of one's death when that method was not even in existence when the prophecy was spoken is indeed amazing. The death of Jesus by crucifixion hundreds of years before the Romans introduced this method of putting criminals to death was foretold by David in Psalm 22:16-18.

Also, these prophecies concerning Jesus are remarkable when viewed from the standpoint of details. Isaiah said that Jesus would be spit on, and David said lots would be cast for Jesus' cloak.

Another remarkable prophecy concerns the death of Jesus. Zechariah said that Jesus would be betrayed for 30 pieces of silver—exactly 30 pieces, no more, no less. How could the prophet possibly have known that exactly 30 pieces would be given to Judas? So remote is the possibility of a coincidence that no honest person would attempt to explain the prophecy on this ground. Only one possible explanation will fit the facts—Zechariah received his knowledge from a divine source. And that is inspiration beyond question.

Therefore, the prophecies given above are impeachable evidence of the truth of inspiration. The how or the method makes but little difference. That God has spoken to men is the great fact to remember. As far as is known, not a single prophecy has failed. If one did fail of fulfillment exactly as predicted—if one length in the chain of divine evidence can be broken, the whole structure will fall to the ground. That the God of the Hebrews, and there is no other, has communicated with man is one of the most stupendous facts of history. These prophecies, therefore, relating to the Jews, to Tyre, to Babylon and to Jesus alone are undeniable proof of the truth that God has spoken to man—and this is inspiration.

CHAPTER THREE

Inspirations—Scientific Evidence

The second line of evidence of the inspiration of Scripture is the scientific foreknowledge of the Biblical writers. Classified knowledge or facts is a simple definition for science. And every fact relating to some specific subject is supposed to be the gospel truth. If it is not true, it is not scientific. Here is what Rev. Weatherhead says on this point: "A sensible modern (person) doesn't expect to find science or accurate history in the Bible." Page 200. The words, "doesn't expect" imply that a sensible person doubts as to whether there is found in the Bible any scientific statements at all. Is this true?

The Bible, it is true, is not a textbook on science. And hundreds of scientific facts and principles are not found in the Bible. However, this is not saying that no scientific facts are given. In truth, the Bible is dotted with such facts.

"Statements of physical and medical science found outside the Bible are twenty to thirty centuries old. Almost out of date is the science taught by Democretus, Ptolemy, Kepler, Galileo, Copernicus and even Newton. Some of the discoveries or deductions taught by these men and regarded as scientific facts have either been proven false or superseded by new discoveries." For example, the earth as taught by Ptolemy was the center of the universe and around it the sun revolved. Now observe—going back hundreds and thousands of years, the science of the Bible was written before the above named scientists were born, "Therefore, by simple logic if near our day what was once believed as scientific facts must be discarded as untrue, then the scientific facts and principles as given in the Bible should have been proven false long ago. Yet the exact opposite is true. Modern scientists have proven that the statements of the Bible relating to science and spoken thousands of years ago are absolutely true. In other words, science is beginning to catch up with the Bible."

Below are examples of scientific statements of the Bible. Only a few out of many will be given. Consider them carefully for here is additional evidence that from a supernatural source has come revealed knowledge to those who wrote the Bible.

Proof from Medicine

In Leviticus 13:46, this verse is found: "He shall remain as long as the disease is in him; he is unclean, he shall live alone, his dwelling outside the camp." According to these instructions, given to Moses and Aaron, a diseased person was to live alone until the disease had run its course. As far as is known, no explanation was given as to why this was necessary. Now grade pupils know that certain diseases are caused by an invisible organism called a germ. And the only safe course to follow to prevent disease from spreading is to isolate the one diseased. Also in the same chapter, detailed instructions are given in regard to the clothing worn by the diseased person. The germs must be destroyed.

Another example is given in Leviticus 7:23. "Say to the Israelites, you shall eat no kind of fat, or wax, or sheep or goat." Again, as far as is known, no explanation for this prohibition is given. Coming from God, the command required only obedience, not explanation. After the command not to eat fat was given 3000 years ago, medical science now knows the reason. In the fat of these animals is found a fatty crystalline alcohol called cholesterol. This substance has an adverse effect upon the heart and is related to the number one killer in the United States—heart disease.

A most intriguing and puzzling question now comes to mind. How could Moses have possibly known these facts? Medical knowledge in ancient times was very limited. And what was believed and practiced was often absurd and stupid. Moses was not guessing when he commanded his people to isolate those diseased, and not to eat the fat of animals. Such knowledge he says himself came from God. This means simply that God did communicate with Moses, and if so this is inspiration.

Proof from Physical Science

Space will permit the giving of only a few examples under this topic. Let us begin with the earth. In ancient and even modern times, scientists maintained that the earth:

1. Was flat.
2. It was stationary.
3. It rested upon an immovable foundation.

With reference to the shape of the earth, Isaiah has this to say: "God sits above the circle of the earth." Circles implies an object that is round. While men were calling the earth flat, Isaiah said it was round. Isaiah 40:22.

A most remarkable statement having to do with the foundation of the earth was made by Job. And it should be remembered that Job is a book of great antiquity. Here it is: "Hangeth the earth on nothing" Job 26:7. That the earth had a solid foundation, we now know was an erroneous concept. Like Job said, it has no foundation at all. Not only was the foundation believed to be solid, it was also immovable. Utterly false we now know was this idea that the earth had a solid foundation and that it was immovable. Job also knew it was false. He declared in 38:14, that the earth turneth as a clay to the seal. Here the idea of motion is stated for the earth is in constant motion around the sun.

Therefore, these scientific statements about the earth—its shape, its constant motion, and it rests on no solid foundation—were known by Job and Isaiah long before they were known by modern man. You tell me, in the far off days in which they lived, how could the prophets have known these facts aside from revelation? And revealed knowledge is inspiration.

Under the topic of physical science, four scientific facts will be given.

1. Science once maintained that in the sky only 1056 stars existed. Revealed by the telescope are untold millions of stars. And it is reasonable to infer that beyond the reach of the telescope are other millions unseen and uncounted. Long, then, before the telescope was even conceived Jeremiah 33:22 stated: "The stars of heaven cannot be numbered." That the stars cannot be numbered is now a known scientific fact.

2. Consider this verse from Job 38:19. "Where is the way where light dwells." Science has discovered some amazing facts about light long after these words were written. Although there are mysteries connected with light that are not yet understood, it is now known that light involves motion. This motion consists of streams of tiny particles or is wave like in its speed. No scientist knows which. And this speed is at the inconceivable rate of 186,000 miles per second. Light, therefore, does not dwell in the sun. The sun is the source of light rays. These rays, as far as is known, will forever continue to move out into space at the same rate. To say, then, that light dwells in the way is a scientific fact.

3. Notice the difference now in a real and apparent motion. As you drive your car down the highway, two motions are involved—one the real and the other an apparent motion. The forward motion of the car is the real motion. The backward motion of the earth is the apparent motion. Watching the sun day after day as it appeared to move across the sky, ancient people were correct in believing the sun was in motion. However, they were wrong in believing this motion was around the earth. For them to mistake the apparent motion of the sun for the real motion was a natural thing to do. Being a member of our galaxy (a vast collection of stars), the sun is moving at some twelve miles per second. The vast circuit prescribed by the sun around some unknown center is now known by astronomers to be true. Now observe—this fact of science was

known by David as given in Psalm 19:6. Therefore, David could say thousands of years before this fact was discovered by modern astronomers; "His going for this from the end of heaven, and his circuit to the end of it." In the absence of a telescope, and not aware of the discoveries of today astronomers, David could have known this fact only from the One who knew it—God. Psalm 19:6.

"Sometimes a Biblical writer will make a casual remark which reveals a wide area of scientific foreknowledge." For example, an electrician may say to a child, "Don't touch that wire. If you do, you may be killed." No explanation concerning the deadly force moving through the wire is made. However, this statement of the electrician would reveal exact knowledge of that force. In the same way, the Bible reveals astonishing foreknowledge of scientific laws. Notice these two examples:

4. Job in 28:25, has this to say: "To make the weight for the winds." Here is an amazing example of a fact of physical science unknown until recent times. No material substance on earth is more familiar than the wind or air. Yet there is no record in existence, as far as I know, of the air having weight before the 17th century. If the idea of the air having weight did occur to great thinkers of the past, there was no way by which this fact could be established. Pascal in the 17th century found a method to prove that air indeed has weight, and in doing so proved Job correct. Thus unknowingly he added one more link to the chain of evidence of the inspiration of the Bible.

5. Another gem revealing two scientific facts is found in Psalm 135:7. "He causeth vapors to ascend from the ends of the earth; He maketh lightnings for the rain." The first part of the above statement—"He causeth vapors to ascend"—refers to evaporation which is a continuous natural process. From one end of the earth to the other, wherever a body of water is found, evaporation goes on. Long after this fact was written, men had no explanation for rainfall. In their ignorance, men once believed that rain came from the moon.

The second fact—"He maketh lightning for the rain"—reveals the relationship between rain and lightning. For hundreds and thousands of years, men have seen the flash of lightning and heard the deep roll of thunder. Yet they did not dream that without the one there could not, in all probabilities, be the other. While the relationship between lightning and rain is not yet fully understood, scientists like Lord Kelvin believe that without lightning there could be no rain. Yet the facts, which are known as to why it rains, move unerringly in the direction of Job's statement, "He maketh lightening for the rain."

Job was not a scientist. Yet in the dim ancient day of long ago, he said that lightning was necessary for rainfall. Unless this fact was revealed to him how could he possibly have known it? To say, therefore, that Biblical writers discovered these scientific facts themselves in the days in which they lived is absurd. Only the God of heaven could have revealed them to them. And this is inspiration.

A further word on the evidence of inspiration from science and we are finished. All the scientific facts enumerated on this topic such as those pertaining to the origin of all life, those relative to the earth, medicine, rainfall, and air could not be verified until the increase of knowledge in modern times. Therefore, they could not have been known by ancient prophets. By no process of research could the prophets have discovered for themselves these facts. Yet they were known. That the prophets wrote of these scientific facts and more is beyond dispute. Only one conclusion, then, is possible. These facts were revealed to them by the Supreme Being who alone knew them. And these revealed facts are inspiration.

Chapter Four

The Bible Speaks for Itself

Let us now turn to the third line of evidence of the inspiration of the Bible. What does the Book say itself with reference to inspiration? Surely its voice has a right to be heard, And if it corroborates the testimony so far given, then a verdict should be rendered in favor of the defendant. First, then, consider a statement by the Apostle Paul who wrote much of the New Testament. Found in Galatians 1:11-12, he declares: "For I want you to know, brethren, that the gospel which was proclaimed and made known by me is not man's gospel—for indeed I did not receive it from man, nor was I taught it; (it came to me) through a (direct) revelation (given) by Jesus Christ, the Messiah."

In these words, Paul insists that what he wrote was communicated to him by Jesus. From men he did not learn what he wrote nor did he in any way receive his message from them. From the above statement, also, one gets the impression that Paul was simply a messenger. From among the hundreds of Christians all mankind, some would receive the message, believe it, and act upon it. Others would deny a part, or all of it, and pass it by.

When Paul wrote the above words, he was either mistaken, lying, or telling the truth. To imply or to state directly that Paul was mistaken about what he wrote in view of the facts will not hold water. Of all the apostles, Paul was the only one who had a formal education. One of the great teachers of Paul's day was Gamaliel, a teacher versed in Jewish law. This man was Paul's teacher according to his own statement in Acts 22:3. Also Acts 21:40 implies that Paul could speak more than one language. Then, too, how can ignorance of the fundamental doctrines of Christianity be ascribed to Paul since Jesus met him on the Damascus Road? From that moment, Jesus through His Spirit became Paul's teacher. Also to catch a glimpse of Paul's knowledge of Christianity, and his power to reason, one has but to read the letters he wrote to the churches. Therefore, Paul was not guessing nor was he ignorant of the truth. Yet this is exactly what Rev. Weatherhead implies, "We are not bound," he says, "to imprison our mind in his theories." By this statement, Weatherhead was referring specifically to Paul's doctrine that without the shedding of blood there is no forgiveness of sins. Hebrews 9:22. When men, therefore, in our day, like Rev. Weatherhead assume to have a greater knowledge of the plan of salvation than did the apostle Paul, they are displaying a colossal amount of egotism.

The second alternative that Paul was lying about the source of the gospel cannot be entertained for a moment. Even before his conversion when persecuting the Christians, he did so believing that no wrong was being done. However, the above statement was written after he had experienced a complete change of character. Overwhelmingly, then, is the evidence that Paul was telling the truth when he insists that his message was revealed to him by Jesus Christ. Therefore, to deny the truth of such statements—"without the shedding of blood there can be no forgiveness of sins"—is to deny also the Source of that message—Jesus Christ.

Turn, now, to 2nd Peter 1:21, and read these words: "For no prophecy ever originated because some man willed it (to do so) it never came by human impulse but as men spoke from God who were borne along (moved, impelled) by the Holy Spirit." Three facts are here mentioned;

1. The forecast or teaching had its origin in the mind of God.
2. The prophet or writer was the messenger.
3. The agency by which the message was made known was the Holy Spirit.

In this age when men are seeking freedom from moral restraint, the personality of the Holy Spirit is being denied. Nevertheless, facts relative to Him in the Scriptures and in human experience are evidence that the Holy Spirit is not some impersonal force or energy, but a real Person of immeasurable power. Therefore, Peter echoes the statement of Paul in that the gospel had its origin in the mind of God. And by means of the enlightenment by the Holy Spirit that Gospel was made known to man.

With reference to the Old Testament writers, two facts will be given concerning their inspiration.

1. In II Timothy 3:16, is found these words: "Every Scripture is God breathed—given by inspiration—." The word "Scripture" applies particularly to the Old Testament. Notice the word, "every." Every Scripture—not just those Rev. Weatherhead thinks are inspired—every principle, idea, event, or fact written by Old Testament writers are inspired and can be trusted, in substance, to be without error,

2. The idea expressed and the events described by Old Testament writers came from one of three sources or from all three. First, they could have originated in their own minds. That is they could have had personal knowledge of a transpired event, or a condition, or circumstance about which they wrote. This, of course, was often true. Second, in some way the Holy Spirit did enlighten their minds, even about things or events of which they had no personal knowledge, to such an extent that all their writing became a reflection of the mind of God.

Surely such men as the writers of the Old Testament were men of honesty and integrity of character. Even the higher critics would not doubt their honesty. Such men, then, as Moses, Isaiah, and Jeremiah says emphatically that their message came from God. Over and over these words are found: "Thus says the Lord," or "the word of the Lord came unto me saying." Rev. Weatherhead says, page 193, that portions of Isaiah, Ezekiel, Jeremiah, and even parts of Paul's writing should be crossed out. For this opinion, he gives two reasons: Either these parts are incomprehensible or are contrary to the Christian spirit or both.

That some portions of the Old Testament and even the New are difficult or beyond our understanding is true. However, for this reason should they be eliminated from the Bible? And is it an indictment against the Book that, due to the dullness of our understanding, we are unable to grasp the truth revealed to us from the Spiritual World? And also is it not a fact that a passage or chapter, the meaning of which is obscure to one person will, upon close scrutiny and study, yield its secrets to another? To say, then, that portions of the Bible should be eliminated because they are difficult or cannot be understood by all makes as much sense as a teacher who would cut out those parts of a text-book which some pupils cannot understand. And last, Paul has something to say on this very point. To the natural man, Paul says, 1 Cor. 2:14, spiritual truths are meaningless. He cannot perceive or discern them clearly. This lack of ability to perceive and recognize the meaning of certain parts of the Scripture explains why some parts of the Scripture cannot be understood by more people.

The second reason given as to some parts of the Scripture should be crossed out is because they are contrary to the Christian spirit. Rev. Weatherhead and those of like mind should not forget that God is a Being not only of love and mercy, but also one of condemnation and judgment. If the treatment of ancient nations and cities seem harsh and cruel by Christian standards as described in the Old Testament, it was only because of the moral degeneration of those nations and cities. Divine justice demanded their destruction.

The assertion, therefore, of Biblical writers that they have, from a Divine source, received or to them have been revealed ideas, principles, and events is evidence of inspiration. Especially is this true, when an event described by them is corroborated by secular history. This corroborating evidence often takes an interesting turn. Hall's handbook of the Bible gives these examples.

In Isaiah 20:1, it says: "Sargon, king of Assyria, sent Tartan and fought against Ashdod and took it." No other ancient literature mentions Sargon's name. For this reason, critics said no such king ever existed. Isaiah, then, had made a statement of an historic fact which was not true. However, in 1842, Botta discovered the ruins of Sargon's palace. An inscription was also found by Sargon verifying exactly what Isaiah had said.

The second example has to do with the city of Nineveh. The prophet Nahum predicted some twenty years before it occurred that Nineveh would be destroyed, and told exactly how the enemy would enter the city. So complete was the destruction that all traces of the Assyrian empire disappeared. In fact, scholars were saying that Nineveh was false. In 1845, the site of Nineveh was discovered. Thousands of clay tablets have been unearthed. On them the history of the Assyrian Empire has been told.

As stated previously, Rev. Weatherhead says that one does not expect to find accurate history in the Bible. Yet archaeology, time and again, has proven the history of the Bible correct and the critics wrong.

Now notice the inspiration of the Bible as compared with the inspiration of other books, if, indeed it can be said that other books are inspired. To repeat, below are two sentences taken from the *Christian Agnostic* found on page 197.

"It is quite true that the Bible is an inspired book, but so are other literary treasures of the world."—

"We need not press for the Bible a different kind of inspiration than which we claim for the great prose and poetry writers of the world. There is only one kind of inspiration."

That there is only one kind of inspiration may be true. However, the question that comes to mind is this: Can it be said that the writers of other great and good books were influenced by the Living Spirit in the same sense as the writers of the Bible? Now notice this difference. Some Biblical writers emphatically insist that their message was not their own. Paul insists that what he wrote, at least in substance, came from Jesus Christ. And the prophets also declared: "Thus saith the Lord." Can you find any book outside the Bible, the writer of which will say that he wrote under the influence of a Divine hand? As stated above, he may have. But if so, the author will not make such a claim. Of the writers of the Bible, a different story can be told. Here they boldly, frankly, and without a sign of boasting or egotism proclaim to the world that the Source of their message, be it history, science, description of events, or some principle of theology, came to them by the enlightenment of the Holy Spirit.

Therefore, the inspiration of the Bible is a fact, This is not saying that minor discrepancies such as a word, tense, singular or plural may not have occurred. But if so, the substance or meaning which the writer meant to convey has not been effected, Evidence, then, upon evidence, proof upon proof has been compiled until there is no room for an honest mind, be he an atheist, infidel, or agnostic, to doubt this glorious truth that the Bible is exactly the book it claims to be. God—the Source of all energy; the Creator of all life; and the Author of moral law—has indeed spoken to the writers of the Bible and through them to the whole human race. Not alone to the race, but to every individual. In this book, He tells me, you, John, and Mary, what He expects of each of us. If one, then, through ignorance, or deliberate rejection will not heed the message, the result is loss of values untold. "Eye has not seen," says Paul, "nor ear heard the things that God has prepared for those who love him."

Chapter Five

The Testimony of Experience

If you are one, who so far has read this manuscript, and still doubts the creditability of the Scriptures, and the authority of Christ to direct your life, then carefully read the next chapter. Additional evidence is given that does not appeal to reason alone—evidence that further substantiates the claim of the Bible as a message to you from God—a message of hope, of help, of instructions, and warnings of impending loss beyond the hope of recovery.

There are many things, in one's environment, that change the character of men. Among these are wealth, power in some form, position, alcohol, drugs, and other people. As far as becoming a better or a worse person, the change then can go either way. There is, however, in the world a Force, Energy or Power that always changes the lives of individuals from a lower to a higher moral plane. To this rule, there are no exceptions. One through the agency of this Power, will inevitably become a better person. This marvelous agency of change, like the force of magnetism, cannot be touched or seen. Its existence is known by the change it effects in the lives of men. Consider, for example, the experience of Melvin Trotter, the evangelist, who was addicted to the use of alcohol. He said:

> "There was not anything in 1897, that I knew about that I had not gone through. I had taken cure after cure. I had taken everything known to science. I had made resolution after resolution. I could no more stay sober than I could fly. When my liberty depended on it, I would lose my liberty because I would break my pledge. I have signed the pledge with my own blood. I promised the judge I would

never drink again, then went right out and did it over again. But one glimpse of Jesus Christ, and I never wanted another drink from that day to this."

To illustrate further the fact that in this world is a matchless Power that changes character, read the story of "Twice Born Men." Here is an authentic account of the religious experiences of the lowest strata of society. Among such men were liars, thieves, pickpockets, and murderers, who experienced that marvelous change of character known in terms of theology as conversion. As proof of the change, they immediately renounced their sinful life. And the author specifically states that the great majority remained true, in spite of fierce temptations, to their love for Christ.

To the validity of such experiences, objections have been raised. Some psychologists have expressed the theory that all such experiences are simply the stirring of the subconscious mind. Most conversions occur in the teens when the sex desire is awakening. However, conversions occur even in old age. And also psychologists now favor the idea that the personality must be considered as a whole, and not the sum total of a number of separate drives. Other psychologists say that mental and spiritual experiences do not exist. They are illusions. What we believe to be real phenomena of the mind and soul are the effects of life as it exists in the body. Every experience can be explained by saying a relationship exists between the mind and the body. And this relationship is such as to cause one to believe that what he thought was an experience was no experience at all. All behavior, then, is some kind of a mechanical process and nothing more.

To this objection the following answer can be given. "While no psychologist will deny that mind and body are related, yet no one can explain the *how* of the relationship. Until this is done, it is only a guess that behavior is nothing more than machine-like action of the body, the power of which is something called life."

Now observe, I have stated that in this world exists a Power that can change for the better the character of any person. And in proof of this examples of criminals, prostitutes, alcohol and drug addicts whose lives be given. However, some may object on the ground that such persons are not reliable witnesses. They are not trained to analyze correctly their own spiritual experiences. That their lives were changed, there is no doubt. However, the power of mind over body and their fierce determination to break some habit or live better lives can account for the change. No outside force or power was involved. To counter this objection, then, we are going to give the testimonies of four great Christian leaders of modern times—Charles G. Finney, Dwight L. Moody, Billy Sunday, and Billy Graham. These four are representatives of those, who throughout the ages, have been instrumental in winning thousands to the ranks of Christianity. Each will speak for himself. Let us begin with Dwight L. Moody.

> "When I came to Christ, I had a terrible battle to surrender my will and take God's will.—If I hated any place before I was converted it was the church. If there was one sound I hated, it was a church bell; but the next morning after I was converted, it was the sweetest sound to me I ever heard. One night the Bible was as dry as last year's almanac. But the next morning it was a new book. The light of heaven shone on every page."
>
> "I was in a new world. The next morning the sun shone brighter and the birds sang sweeter, the old elms waved their branches in joy, and all nature was at peace. It was the most delicious joy I have ever known. *They Call Him Mister Moody* (pages 53-54).

Here is Billy Graham's description of an event which changed the direction of his life.

> "Have you ever been outside on a dark day when the sun suddenly burst through the clouds? Deep

inside that's how I felt. But the next day, I am sure, I looked the same. But to me everything, even the flowers and the leaves on the trees, looked different. I was finding out for the first time the sweetness and joy of God, of being truly born again." *Billy Graham, High* (page 36).

Of his conversion, Billy Sunday, who persuaded thousands to decide for Christ, has this to say:

"I walked down a street with other ball players who were famous in this world, some are dead now, and we went into a saloon. It was Sunday afternoon and we got tanked up and then went and sat down on a street corner. I never go by that street without thanking God for saving me. Across the street a company of men and women were playing on instruments and singing hymns I used to hear in Sunday school. I arose and said to the boys: 'I'm through, I am going to Jesus Christ. We have come to a parting of the ways.' Some laughed, some mocked, some spoke encouraging, and others never said a word." *The Sawdust Trail* (pages 16-19, 20).

Of all great evangelists both in America and abroad, perhaps Charles G. Finney stands at the head of the list. A Christian leader of incomparable greatness, no minister of modern times has outranked Finney as a vehicle through whom the Spirit convicted men of sin. Space will permit only a few excerpts of his testimony in finding his way to God.

"Just at that point (Finney at this time, a twenty-seven-year-old attorney, was praying in a piece of woods north of the village in which he lived), this passage of scripture seemed to drop into my mind with a flood of light:

" 'Then shall ye seek me and find me, when ye shall search for me with all your heart.'

"Somehow I knew that that was a passage of scripture, though I do not think I had ever read it. (This passage is found in Jer. 29:12.) I knew it was

God's Word and God's voice, as it were, that spoke to me. I cried to Him, 'Lord I take Thee at Thy word—' There was no fire, and no light in the room; nevertheless it appeared to me as if it was perfectly light. As I went in and shut the door after me, it seemed as if I met the Lord Jesus Christ face to face. It did not occur to me then that it was wholly a mental state. I fell down at His feet and wept like a child and made such confessions as I could with my choked utterance. As soon as my mind became calm enough to break off the interview, I returned to the front office, but as I turned and was about to take a seat by the fire, the Holy Spirit descended upon me in a manner that seemed to go through my body and soul. I could feel the impressions, like waves of electricity going through and through me. No words can express the wonderful love that was shed abroad in my heart. I wept aloud with joy and love." *Memoirs of Charles G. Finney* (pages 16-19-12).

Notice that of these four conversions, one like Finney's was accompanied with intense emotion, while that of Billy Sunday was characterized by a definite clear-cut decision in which but little or no emotion was involved. Notice, too, that not only those of low moral character, but those of the highest like the four great leaders mention, attribute their change of character to God or Jesus Christ. Now personally, Christ is not on this earth. He does have a Representative here that works and speaks for Him. To identify that Representative turn to John 15:26, 16:7-13. Here, then, we are told that the agency of spiritual experiences is a living Person know as the Holy Spirit. People, then, in all walks of life from the highest to the lowest testify to a change of character. Here among men, in our day, is a profound alteration of conduct that can be explained on no other ground. The Living Spirit of Christ, then, is as much in evidence today as He was when first spoken of 2000 years ago—the same Spirit that moved the heart of thousands on the day of Pentecost. And these experiences are additional evidence of the inspiration of the Bible.

CHAPTER SIX

Evidence of the Virgin Birth

The objections to the truth of the stories of the virgin birth by Luke and Matthew have been discussed. Notice that the answers to these objections have depended entirely upon the truthfulness of Matthew and Luke. And if no one rejected their testimony, it would not be necessary to go further. Their word, which no doubt would be accepted in a court of law, would be final.

However, those who deny the virgin birth are really saying that Matthew, Luke and others of the apostles whose writings indirectly tend to substantiate Luke's narrative of Jesus' birth, are not telling the truth. This could be due, not so much to a deliberate resolve to falsify the facts as, to a mistaken belief that they were writing a true account of His birth. Yet if they incorporated in their gospels accounts of His birth some idea from the imagination of a Greek author—a mixture of what was true or false—they certainly were not reliable reporters of the life of Jesus. The problem, then, is to determine, if that is possible, the reliability of Matthew and Luke.

There are two ways this can be done. One is to discover from their past conduct if they were honest and dependable. The other is to verify their stories. Of course, it is impossible to investigate fully the life of Matthew and Luke. This can be done, however, to a certain degree. Evidence that not only does God exist but also He has communicated with the authors of the Bible has been given in a previous chapter. I believe that it is not too strong a statement to say that much of this evidence is well nigh irrefutable. Matthew and Luke were Bible writers, therefore they were inspired men. If all skeptics would accept this fact, they would no longer question the accuracy of Luke's story and this discussion would end right here. However, since inspiration is denied, this evidence is of no value to those who refuse to accept it.

Let us now take a look at some truths which are difficult to deny. A man, then, whose name was Jesus actually was born some 2000 years ago. The evidence of this is so all inclusive that only half-hearted attempts have been made to deny it. Second, the deity of Jesus, His sinless, His resurrection, and of course His miracles—all have about them a common factor. And that factor is a miraculous element or quality. Third, these things cannot apply to any other man. No man, for example, as a man has ever performed a miracle. Men alone just don't perform miracles in the strict sense of that word. No man has ever risen from the dead who did not die again. No man can lay claim to divinity as was reported of Jesus Christ. It is such factors that binds together these events of Jesus' life and character. There is, therefore, a connection or unity between all of them. Every miracle it is reported He performed required the force of a supernatural power; His sinlessness and deity if true are attributes of a God; and His resurrection demanded a type of life over which death had no power. All these are bound together by a divine force which no man can duplicate. If, due to this unity, it can be proven that one is true, all then will be true. And if one is false, all are false. And this in turn leads directly to the Virgin Birth.

It should be observed also that to be consistent one must accept all as true or all as false. Rev. Weatherhead, for example, accepts as true the resurrection but denies some miracles. It seems to me that here is an inconsistency in accepting some miracles as true but denying others as false. The modernists are certainly being consistent when they deny all miracles.

To arrive at the truth, as far as the truth can be determined, let us begin with the resurrection. The internal evidence of the resurrection, as given in the gospels, depends on the testimony of eye-witnesses. With reference to this evidence, those who deny the resurrection are simply saying that those who say they saw Him are either lying or were mistaken. Or the apostles—Matthew, Mark, Luke, and John—either manufactured these witnesses from their imagination, or they were unreliable in reporting a lie told by others or what others thought was true. If one does not, then, believe the resurrection this is the only conclusion at which one can arrive.

There are three lines of inquiry which can be pursued concerning the truth of the resurrection. They are:

1. Testimony of the four gospels.
2. Testimony of Paul.
3. Testimony of experience.

With reference to the first, volumes have been written concerning these gospel accounts. Every word, phrase, and sentence have been scrutinized as it were with a magnifying glass in an attempt to find flaws in these accounts. Only briefly can these accounts be touched on here. The four central facts told by all four of the gospels writers (details will differ) are listed below.

1. The manner of Christ's death.
2. The place of burial.
3. The length of that burial.
4. The resurrection.

These facts and all the details connected with them if it could be shown were written from hearsay would be discounted at once. However, the men who tell us about these awful events lived at the time they occurred. They were on the scene and all four were in one way or another, they tell us, actors in an incredible living drama, the scenes of which were occurring before their eyes. Writing a clear, concise account, they gave not only the events surrounding the resurrection, but also such details as names, time, places, and conversation between the characters. The author who wrote the book, *Who Moved the Stone?* set out with the purpose of proving the resurrection false. After a careful study of the details of the narratives as given by the four gospel writers, he came to accept these narratives as the truth and the resurrection as a fact.

All the gospel writers, then, declare they themselves saw Jesus and talked with Him after He arose from the tomb, except Luke. However, their testimony does not stand alone; many others as reported by them saw Jesus also. As stated by John, Mary Magdalene saw Jesus and talked with Him on the morning of the resurrection. Luke says that Jesus appeared to two men on the road to Emmaus. In fact as many as 500 saw Him at one time and looked upon the face of the Man who alone of all men rose from the dead to die no more.

Now here is a peculiar thing with reference to these witnesses who saw Jesus after His resurrection. What would have been a more convincing testimony of proof that Jesus arose from the dead than that of His enemies? He could have appeared to those who sent Him to the cross in such a manner that it would have been known far and wide. Had He done so, they would have been forced to admit it, thus proving even to His enemies that His resurrection was a fact. When a man admits a truth that is to his interest to conceal, there is no question as to the truth of that fact. If the four gospels were pure fabrication, in whole or in part, would not the four writers have included the testimony of those who condemned Jesus to the Cross? What greater evidence could they have manufactured to prove that Jesus rose from the dead than that of His enemies who at all cost did want the truth known? Yet we have no such testimony. None is given because Jesus did not appear to His enemies. Or if He did, it is not recorded. The lack of testimony to the resurrection from those who passed the sentence of death upon Him is itself evidence that they wrote a true account of the resurrection.

As reported, then, by the apostles, here on record is not only their only testimony to the resurrection but that of many others of their day. On the one hand is an incredible event—

one that never happened before or since—so unbelievable that men of strong intellect cannot accept it as true. On the other hand, is what appears to be unshakable testimony that the event is true just as it is recorded. If you doubt, like Fosdick, the truth of the resurrection, reserve a final judgment until all the evidence is in.

Turn now to the testimony of Paul. If the character of a witness can be impeached, his testimony is of little or no value. If, however, he is known to be reliable and trustworthy, his testimony will carry great weight. Consider, then some facts with reference to the character of the apostle Paul. Paul wrote the letters that bear his name with the possible exception of Hebrews. This statement to my knowledge has never been questioned. Today these letters can be read and studied by anyone as they form a large part of the New Testament. His writings, therefore, tells us much about the character of one of the greatest of Christ's apostles. First, they reveal his love, loyalty, and devotion to Jesus. Since the rankest of His enemies could not with truth accuse Jesus of wrong doing, how could Paul be loyal and devoted to Him and at the same time be deceitful and untruthful? This could be possible only on the assumption that Paul was a rank hypocrite. When other facts are considered, this just can't be true. Second, these letters reveal that Paul was a man of high intelligence, great learning, keen judgment, and that he possessed the ability to reason in a clear logical manner. If you would obtain a keen insight into Paul's knowledge of human nature, man's great spiritual needs, and how those needs can be met, read the 8th chapter of Romans and the 13th chapter of 1 Corinthians.

Now I ask the question: would such a man fabricate an event or an experience that did not occur as he related it? You know that he would not. Paul, then, has something definite to tell us about the resurrection of Jesus. In the 9th chapter of Acts, he states how Jesus met him on the Damascus Road. A clear, detailed description of what occurred is there given. The chief facts are these: Paul was suddenly arrested on his journey by a bright light that shone around him. Then to his astonishment, a voice spoke which identified itself as that of Jesus. He was told exactly what he must do. Yet the central fact of this encounter with Jesus was not the voice nor the light but rather an inner change of character. His whole attitude toward Christ and the Christians of his day was completely changed. One moment he was determined to wipe out the whole Christian sect, the next he found himself on the side of those whom he would destroy. During the remainder of his life, his personal love and loyalty for Jesus never wavered even in the face of great suffering and bitter hardships.

In view, then, of what is known about the character of Paul, his testimony must be true. The voice that spoke to him was that of Jesus. And if there is one fact which calls for rejoicing it is this, that Jesus is alive *now*. He lives behind the veil that divides the spiritual from the physical world. And the fact that He must have known Paul long before Paul knew Him, is evidence that He not only knows each one of us but is intensely interested in us.

The third line of evidence is that from experience. And it may appear rather far-fetched to declare that the testimony of experience is evidence of an event that occurred almost 2000 years ago. Yet if an experience today so profound that it results in a change of attitude, affections, and ways of thinking—in short a change of character—depends upon an event that occurred 2000 years ago, then this is proof positive that the event actually took place. It is not our purpose to enter into a philosophical speculation as to the validity of religious experiences. To show the connection between a change in the direction of life by such an experience and the resurrection, all that is necessary is to consider some actual cases.

Suppose we start with my own experience. Just as John said who wrote one of the gospels that his testimony was true so what I am going to relate is true also. I simply would not be telling the truth if I said otherwise. While still in my teens, I attended, in a schoolhouse, the first revival meeting in my life. Each night for two weeks, moved by some inner force or power, I knelt, at what was called in those days the mourners' bench. I prayed and wept while others sought to help me to gain whatever it was I was seeking. What kept me seeking was this inner drive. I know now the explanation of that urge that gently but firmly moved me in the direction of God. On the last night, I became fearful and desperate that the meeting would close with no real peace. Suddenly there swelled up within me a peace, joy, and love which before I had never felt. Two physical reactions occurred immediately. First, in a moment without taking any thought as to my actions, I threw my arms around a girl kneeling on my left. Second, my face, I was told afterward, shone as by some inner light. Now notice two facts relative to this experience. First, it was no emotional upheaval that soon vanished like fog in a morning sun. The intensity of the experience did wane as the days and months went by. Yet I must say, in the interest of truth, that a quiet peace has followed me from that day to this and an inner conviction that no matter what happens everything is going to be all right. There is no other explanation I can give or can be given for these effects which had their beginning at an altar of prayer.

Before that final night of the meeting, I had given but little thought to Christ. To me He was just another great man like Lincoln or Washington. Suddenly this attitude changed. A love for Him such as I have never felt for no other person swelled up within me. And this supreme affection has never departed from me.

Is such an experience as I have described unique with me? No, not by any means. And to corroborate this answer, below are given three quotations of four great modern Christian leaders. These are Charles G. Finney, Dwight L. Moody, Billy Sunday, and Billy Graham. These five, including myself, are representatives of Christians of all ages and in all walks of life.

"When I came to Christ, I had a terrible battle to surrender my will and take God's will—If I hated any place before I was converted it was the church. If there was one sound I hated—it was—a church bell; but the next morning after I was converted, it was the sweetest sound to me I ever heard. One night the Bible was as dry as last year's almanac. But the next morning it was a new book. The light of heaven shown on every page.—I was in a new world. The next morning the sun shone brighter and the birds sang sweeter—the old elms waved their branches in joy, and all nature was at peace. It was the most delicious joy I have ever known."(*They call Him Mr. Moody,* pages 53-54.)

"Have you ever been outside on a dark day when the sun suddenly burst through the clouds? Deep inside that's how I felt. But the next day, I am sure, I looked the same. But to me everything even the flowers and the leaves on the trees looked different. I was finding out for the first time the sweetness and joy of God, of being truly born again." (*Billy Graham,* page 36.)

"I walked down a street with other ball players who were famous in this world—some are dead now—and we went into a saloon. It was Sunday afternoon and we got tanked up and then went and sat down on a street corner. I never go by that street without thanking God for saving me.—Across the street a company of men and women were playing on instruments—and singing hymns—I used to hear in Sunday school. I arose and said to the boys: 'I'm through. I am going to Jesus Christ. We have come to a parting of the ways'—some laughed, some mocked, some spoke encouraging, and others never said a word." (*The Sawdust Trail,* pages 16-20.)

Of all great evangelists both in America and abroad, perhaps Charles G. Finney stands at the head of the list. A Christian leader of incomparable greatness, no minister of modern times has out-ranked Finney as a vehicle through who the Spirit convicted men of sin.

"Just at this point (Finney at this time was a twenty-seven-year-old attorney praying in a piece of woods north of the village in which he lived) this passage of Scripture seemed to drop into my mind with a flood of light: 'Then shall ye go and pray unto me, and I will hearken unto you. Then shall ye seek me and find me, when ye shall search for me with all your heart.'—Somehow I knew that was a passage of Scripture, though I do not think I had ever read it. (This passage is found in Jeremiah 29:12.) I knew it was God's Word and God's voice, as it were, that spoke to me. I cried to Him, 'Lord I take thee at Thy word.'—There was no fire, and no light in the room; nevertheless it appeared to me as if it was perfectly light. As I went in and shut the door after me, it seemed as if I met the Lord Jesus Christ face to face. It did not occur to me then—that it was wholly a mental state.—I fell down at His feet—and wept like a child and made such confessions as I could with my choked utterance.—As soon as my mind became calm enough to break off the interview, I returned to the front office—But as I turned and was about to take a seat by the fire—the Holy Spirit descended upon me in a manner that seemed to go through my body and soul. I could feel the impressions, like waves of electricity going through and through me.—No words can express the wonderful love that was shed abroad in my heart. I wept aloud with joy and love."

Let us analyze these experiences and see what conclusions can be drawn from them. Observe that no two are the same in all details. However, there are factors that are common to all. These are:

    1. All in some way mention Christ. Finney saw Him as in a vision; Billy Sunday said he was going to

Christ; Moody used about the same expression; and Billy Graham used the word God instead of Christ.
2. All, except Rev. Sunday, either in describing their experience used the words peace, joy, and love, or stated a condition of mind which implied they felt these emotions.
3. The most pronounced result of their experiences was a change in the direction of their lives. This really amounted to a change in character, and a love and peace which only the presence of Christ can produce.

The resurrection of Jesus is, therefore, a fact of history. The testimony of the inner circle of His disciples, the testimony of those of His day, outside that circle, the testimony of Paul, and the testimony today of Christians in all walks of life form a body of evidence of Christ's resurrection which is most difficult to reject. In fact if the question of His resurrection was decided in a court of law, the verdict, in all probabilities, would be in the affirmative. One thing remains to be done—connect His resurrection with His virgin birth.

Even though I know that Jesus is alive today, yet about His resurrection there are elements of mysteries which baffle explanation. However, this is known, His resurrection proves beyond doubt that Jesus possessed a life which in its nature is eternal. This means He had life within Himself, and unlike human life it did not depend on an environment. Death, over such a life, has no power. If this was not true, He could not have risen from the dead. This is known since no other man has ever come forth from the grave except by an outside power and then to die again. On the other hand, Jesus died a physical death—the machinery of His body stopped for a time, only to resume operation when He arose to die no more. Now notice, if Jesus had an earthly father, like other men, He would have possessed only human life. This being true, He would not or could not have risen from the grave. Men do not come forth from the grave to die no more. The question now is how can such a life as that possessed by Jesus be accounted for? Since Jesus was a man, from a natural point of view, His life should not have possessed a quality that could bridge the grave. Viewing then, the question from every angle, and bringing into focus every known fact, there is only one way by which to account for a life such as Jesus possessed. Only the eternal God then, could have been His Father. His resurrection is therefore, proof of His virgin birth.

In view of these two great historical facts—His Virgin birth and His resurrection—it is useless to seek evidence in support of the sinlessness of Jesus, His deity, His miracles, and His pre-existence. All these disputed doctrines now fall within the range of possibility. The virgin birth establishes beyond question that Jesus was not just another great and good man. There was within Him, since the virgin birth is true, an element of Divinity. That He, then, in some explicable way was both God and man has long been an accepted truth of the Christian world. As a man He could not, of Himself, have performed any miracle. As a God, the changing of water to wine, stilling a tempest, healing all kinds of diseases, and raising the dead were simple things for Him to have done.

The same line of reasoning applies to His deity, His sinlessness, and His pre-existence. The gospel writers report that Jesus Himself said that He lived before coming to the earth, and that He was without sin. However, there are those who will not accept, as true, their report. Yet corroborating these reports are the facts of His resurrection and virgin birth. An honest seeker after truth, in the light of the evidence given, will accept His virgin birth. This in turn means that all the apostles wrote about Jesus is true.

CHAPTER SEVEN
Why Men Disbelieve the Gospel

Why, it may be asked, do men of intelligence, education, and moral integrity refuse to accept as true these doctrines which are obviously a part of the gospel? Not only in modern but also in ancient times, they have been called in question. Many answers, perhaps, could be given. Below are four which in part, at least, will answer the question.

1. No reasonable explanation can be given for the event or done at all. Those who hold this view insist that the Virgin Birth, the resurrection, and the miracles, for examples, contradict not only one's reason but also the laws of nature. To such men as Rev. Weatherhead and Dr. Barclay whom he quotes on page 117, the ability to think, to form ideas, to retain events, to form judgments—in short to reason—is the only tool for discovering the truth. And in dealing with physical things, such as objects both alive and dead, reason is the chief tool for discovering facts in the material realm. However, there exists a realm of facts or truths which the light of reason cannot wholly illuminate. I refer to that other realm known as the Spiritual World from which Christianity has come. To know fully all such truths, they must be revealed by experience. Now the tool or the chief tool by which spiritual truths are known or experienced is obedience, John 7:17. It is at this very point where so many men have gone astray. They use the tool or instrument of reason to discover facts which can only be found by obedience. Since this subject will be dealt with in a separate paper, I can only say here that in fact both reason and obedience can be used to discover the truth in both the physical and spiritual worlds. Then, too, reason alone should tell any honest seeker after the truth that a gospel, not in part but in whole, is true

that can change, when obeyed, the heart of the liar, the thief, or the murderer. Take, for example, this passage found in 9:22 of Hebrews. If this passage is not true, then the whole sacrificial idea of the death of Jesus is false. By using his intelligence or reason one can amass evidence for and against the truth of the passage. Suppose now one uses also the other tool for discovering the truth—obedience. This can be done by one confessing his sins and in all honesty seeking enlightenment from a Divine source, by seeking instruction from a Christian friend or minister, or as is often done, by kneeling in church at a public altar. Whether you believe the Bible is an inspired book or not and has back of it the authority of God, makes no difference at this point. The whole idea is that you are combining reason with obedience to discover the truth. Try this and keep on trying, and like the soft rays of the sun as they fall upon the earth, peace and enlightenment will come to your dark and troubled mind.

2. A second reason why the Bible as an inspired book in whole or in part is rejected is the simple fact that evidence pertaining to the other side is ignored. A university student rejected the inspiration and what to her were unreasonable teaching of the Bible. She was given material that contained evidence which proved she was wrong. She refused to even read it. This refusal pointed straight to the fact that she did not want to know the truth. Such an attitude is merely another form of dishonesty. Then there are those who will read or listen to the other side, but they will not honestly consider the evidence. This was exactly the position of the Jews in regard to Jesus. "If you will not," He told them, "believe that I am the Messiah, then accept what I am doing for only a Divine Person could do these things." Here was clear-cut indisputable evidence before their eyes that Jesus was what He claimed to be. Yet as far as is known, the Jews did not stop to even examine the evidence.

The same unreasonable and dishonest refusal to consider the evidence is as true today as it was in the time of Jesus.

Take, for example, just one single line of evidence of the truth of inspiration—prophecy. Here is evidence beyond dispute. I have never heard or read of a doubter, atheist, or infidel who has even attempted to deny it with any degree of success. Some have argued that the event occurred *before* the prophecy was made. However, such an idea can, in so many of the prophecies, be proven false without difficulty that the argument is not worthy of consideration. Now notice—there is no way by which prophecy can be proven false. The method used, then, by the atheist, or doubter is just to ignore it. This is exactly the method used by Rev. Weatherhead. Nowhere in his book will you find a discussion of this topic. Therefore, ignoring or refusing to honestly consider the evidence, in favor, for example of, the Virgin Birth or "blood atonement of Jesus" is another reason why the Bible is not regarded as an inspired book.

3. That a man wants to live his life in his own way, without restrictions even from God, is a factor in his rejection of some Biblical teachings. With respect to this idea, only two alternatives are possible. Either I direct the affairs of my life according to the dictates of the self, or by an act of will I direct them according to the dictates of an another Person—Jesus Christ.

However, when one begins to consider his conduct on the one hand, and the teachings of Christ on the other, a conflict of more or less intensity issues between what I *want* to do and what I *ought* to do. Consider the relation between the sexes. Jesus approves sex relation only between those who are married. However, such a command limits one's freedom of action. The same things can be said of one's methods of making money. Christ's teachings as well as those of the apostles are squarely against cheating and dishonesty in all its forms. Again in the methods of making money, one's freedom of action is limited. The result, then, of this conflict between Jesus and the desire of the "self" to have its own way is a faint inner warning, a vague uneasiness that all is not well. Then you take refuge in certain ideas which allow greater scope of action, and at the same time bring a degree of peace to your troubled mind. Some of these ideas are:

1. When Jesus speaks of retribution, punishment, or loss, He really was misquoted or He did not make the statement at all. For example, Matthew says Jesus will divide the good people from the bad or the sheep from the goats, and the bad are to go into everlasting punishment. Rev. Weatherhead tells us that Jesus did not make this statement, page 90. For Jesus to have done so is not like Him at all, or such words are entirely out of keeping with His character. If Rev. Weatherhead is right, then, his views ought to be especially comforting to the adulterous husband or wife; the cheating, crooked business man; or the dictator who, for sake of power, takes human life when no one can call him to account.

2. Since it is impossible for a man to be born without a father, the Virgin Birth cannot be true. And since it is not true, Jesus is just another man. Therefore, He has no more authority to tell me what to do or not to do than any other man.

3. There are, we are told, by those who accept the "new liberal morality"—no absolute principles of right or wrong. This idea stems from a belief that no God exists, and the view which is taken of man himself. "Therefore, today many non-Christian intellectuals believe that man is not truly a person in the full sense of the word. They look upon him as an unexplainable element in this chance-produced world, and deny the reality of man's freedom to make choices. They insist that what he does and thinks is completely under the control of chemical processes within his body or psychological factors to which he has been subjected." If, then, a man lies, steals, or commits murder, he has really done no wrong since he was subjected to certain forces within him and without over which he has no control. Therefore, he is not responsible for his conduct. For this reason, then, the robber and the adulterer reject the Bible as untrue because it does hold him responsible for his conduct.

There is, therefore, no such thing as rigid, unchanging moral law which, of course cannot be true. To steal now is as much a violation law as it was 1,000 years ago.

4. As an experience which changes for the better the lives of men, none transcends in importance the New Birth. It is, then, our contention that the majority of those who deny the Virgin Birth, the resurrection, the miracles, the Divinity of Jesus, and the inspiration of the Bible do not know from experience the meaning of conversion. Of all the reasons given as to why men of intelligence, education, and theological training reject the above teachings of the Bible, this is the greatest. In making this statement, I am not directly or by inference judging such persons. By the word *judging* here is meant passing sentence. Passing sentence upon one's beliefs, conduct, and relationship to Christ is a prerogative which belongs to Him alone. Nevertheless when certain teachings of the Bible are denied and these same teachings have changed the lives of millions including some of the wickedest of men, I have the right to question as to whether such men have a vital living relationship to Jesus Christ. For further discussion, suppose again we list those great Biblical teaching which Rev. Weatherhead, and others of like mind either doubt or outright deny.

1. The story of the Virgin Birth of Jesus as given in the gospels.
2. Some of the miracles which Jesus is reported to have performed.
3. Divine forgiveness is not possible without the shedding of blood.
4. The inspiration of the Bible in the sense that the Holy Spirit especially enlightened the minds of those who wrote it.
5. Personality of the Holy Spirit.
6. Divinity and sinlessness of Jesus.
7. As a result of deliberate rejection of Jesus as one's personal Saviour, eternal separation from God which is Hell.

Now notice—the criteria or way by which a principle or teaching is judged is does it work. Does the teaching or belief, when acted upon, change for the better the character of a man? If no change occurs or if the change is not for the better, then that belief, principle or teaching should be discarded. With reference, then, to this criteria, I am going to give a brief account of the conversion, beliefs, and accomplishments of some of the great leaders of Christianity. Then compare their accomplishments with those who deny the seven doctrines listed above. Let us begin with John Wesley.

1. Rev. Wesley had been preaching for some time when one evening there came to him a deeper experience in his relation to Christ. Let Rev. Wesley tell about it himself. "In the evening May 24, 1738, I went very unwillingly to a meeting in Alder Street where one was reading a Luther's preface to the Epistle to the Romans. At 15 minutes till nine, while he was describing the change which God works in the heart through Christ, I felt my heart strangely warmed. I felt I trust in Christ alone for my salvation." Notice Rev. Wesley pinpoints the exact time when the mysterious supernatural change occurred.

The full result of Rev. Wesley's work in persuading men of his day to follow Christ cannot be known this side of eternity. As founder of the great Methodist Church, his influence in changing, for the better, the character of men still goes on. In a sense, men change men. However, when the change is for good, and man alone is the agency, the resulting change is not transformation but reformation. When the Holy Spirit is the agency and man is the instrument used by the Spirit, the resulting change is not reformation but transformation. When Rev. Wesley had been transformed by the renewing of his mind through the agency of the Holy Spirit, the character of hundreds and thousands were changed by his ministry.

His beliefs and teachings were strictly along Biblical lines. As far as I have been able to determine, John Wesley accepted as the true inspiration of the Bible, Christ's atonement, and all the doctrines which modern day liberals deny. Rev. Weatherhead denies that any man, though he be a Hitler, will be eternally separated from God. In the far off reaches of eternity, he insists that men, though they set their wills like flint against Christ and all He stands for, will in eternity if not in time be brought in union with the Father. Rev. Wesley, who preached one sermon on future punishment, says it is not true. And a greater than Wesley, Jesus Christ, said the same thing.

2. Dwight L. Moody, the great American Evangelist, is well known to the people of this generation. As in the case of any great change in character, a period of preparation always precedes the moment of actual change. The soil or the moral nature must be broken up in preparation for receiving the seed known as the Christ-life. This was true in the case of Mr. Moody. By attending church, Sunday school, and by Bible study, he was being prepared, for that April day (21st) 1855. On this day, Edward Kimball, Moody's Sunday school teacher, made a momentous decision. Kimball went to the shoe store where Moody was working. Placing his hand on the young man's shoulder, he told Moody of Christ's love for him and the love Christ wanted in return. From that hour, Moody was a changed man. A new power which brought assurance, peace, and a radical change of mind had entered his soul. Notice also that in his biography is recorded the exact day and year when this marvelous change occurred.

With reference to those seven doctrines listed above, I can find no hint that Rev. Moody rejected any of them. He did not cease, throughout the long years of his ministry, to preach the vicarious suffering of Christ. To him the blood atonement, which even ministers today reject with scorn, he taught as a fact. To him, also, Jesus was not only a man but God also clothed in human flesh. This great preacher, whose heart was changed by the Living Spirit, unlike Rev. Weatherhead, believed and taught that the writers of the gospels gave an accurate and true account of the birth, life, teaching, and death of Jesus.

To properly evaluate Rev. Moody's work is not possible for the influence of the life he lived is still going on. He preached to thousands in great meetings held in many parts of the country.

3. The third Christian leader of incomparable greatness was Charles G. Finney. If ever a man in modern times served as a vehicle for the expression of the Holy Spirit, that man was Finney. He was born August 24, 1792 at Warren, Connecticut. On August 16, 1875, he died. Reckoning from the year of his conversion 1821, to the day of his death, he preached the gospel for some fifty-four years.

In his autobiography, he gives the account of the events leading up to a most remarkable experience. No religious experience of which I have any knowledge can compare with it except that which came to the 120, on the day of Pentecost. To relate a brief account, Finney, who was a twenty-seven-year-old lawyer, became deeply agitated about his spiritual condition. On a Tuesday morning, he slipped away to a deep woods near his home. Without a knowledge of the passing of time, he was on his knees in prayer, and greatly troubled in spirit from morning till noon. Then a quite peace stole over his troubled soul like that which results after a passing storm. Let Mr. Finney continue the narrative as given in the *Memoirs of Charles G. Finney,* page 20.

> "But as I turned and was about to take a seat by the fire, I received a mighty baptism of the Holy Spirit. Without any expectation of it, without ever having the thought in mind that there was any such thing in mind for me, without any recollection that I had ever heard the thing mentioned by any person in the world, the Holy Spirit descended upon me in a manner that seem to go through me, body and soul. I could feel the impressions, like a wave of electricity, going through and through me. Indeed it seems to come in waves and waves of liquid love; for I could not express it in any other way. It seemed like the breath of God. I can recollect distinctly that it

seemed to fan me, like immense wings. No words can express the wonderful love that was shed abroad in my heart. I wept aloud with joy and love."

Now I would like to ask Rev. Weatherhead, what was it that swept over Finney like the fanning of immense wings? Was it an influence or some blind energy or force? There was an energy involved but it was an energy the source of which was a Person. Jesus Himself by using the pronouns "Him" and "He" said that the Holy Spirit was a Person, for Him and He are pronouns that refer only to a person. Also in the light of what followed, Finney's baptism involves intelligence. And intelligence is always associated with a person. Finney was being prepared by a Divine Power for the work that lay before him. Only the Living Spirit of God can change character. And that Spirit since the day of Pentecost does not make His presence felt or He does not come directly to a person, but uses people as a vehicle of expression. He moves from heart to heart, or through one person to another person. In Finney, then, the Spirit found a man, judging from results, that was an almost perfect instrument for His purposes. Intelligence, then, was shown not only by the man He choose, but also by the timing involved. The clouds of civil war were gathering over the nation. Hundreds and thousands of young men would be wounded or die on the battlefields. To prepare not only the thousands who would die but those who would not in the coming struggle God needed a leader, and that leader was Finney. 500,000 conversions, it has been said, could be traced to Finney's ministry and a surprising number of the 500,000 were young men.

An account of Mr. Finney's profound religious experience, and a brief account of his work has been given. Turn now to the doctrines or teachings upon which that work was based. On pages 77 and 134 of his memoirs, these doctrines will be found. Here they are: The atonement of Jesus, His Divinity, His perfect life or sinlessness, His vicarious death, His resurrection, the personality of the Holy Spirit, eternal punishment (page 120), and His humanity. While no direct references to them are made, there is no doubt that Finney accepted as true the inspiration of the Bible as a revelation from God, the Virgin Birth of Jesus, and His miracles. Finney, therefore, believed as true every one of those seven doctrines that Rev. Weatherhead doubts or rejects as false. And remember that Finney like the apostles on the day of Pentecost, and many others, was baptized in a most remarkable way by the Holy Spirit. And also Finney states time and again how the Spirit taught him facts about the gospel, and opened up to his mind ideas which were especially needed in his preaching. Now would not this Spirit have taught Finney not to teach those seven doctrines if they were not true? And conversely since Rev. Weatherhead doubts or denies them, is not this evidence that in his relation to Christ that something is badly missing?

These three Christian leaders—John Wesley, Dwight L. Moody, and Charles G. Finney—are typical of those Christian leaders who have emerged in modern times. Among these are: Martin Luther, George Whitefield, Gypsy Smith, Billy Sunday, Charles G. Spurgeon, and Billy Graham. Some if not all of these great evangelists can pinpoint, the year, month, day, and even hour when their lives were changed by an inexplicable spiritual experience known as the New Birth.

Two very interesting and important facts should now be noticed. First, all of these evangelists and others taught as true those seven doctrines listed above. Before their spiritual experience, they may have been indifferent to them or even were atheists or infidels. Let that be as it may, the fact remains that afterward all doubts were swept away and these doctrines came to be regarded as of the utmost importance if not the very heart of the gospel. To them, the Bible is an inspired book and that in a sense that cannot be said of any other book as Rev. Weatherhead contends; the Holy Spirit is not some influence but a Person who knows each one by name; Paul's statement that without the shedding of blood there is no remission of sin is accepted without question; and the Virgin Birth they regard as a fact. Second, in the field of science, the test of an idea, is does it work? This fact holds true with reference to those seven great doctrines of the gospel. The result which followed the belief in and the teaching of these doctrines by the ministers of the gospel has turned millions to Jesus Christ.

Therefore, those who have experienced the joy and peace of mind through Divine forgiveness know that Jesus was or is more than man, and that their forgiveness is possible or that they have no difficulty in believing that He died for them. There is knowledge or belief that transcends reason. That person in whom the Holy Spirit has taken His abode will be taught by Him. "—He will teach you all things and bring all things to your remembrance, whatsoever I have said unto you." The man, then, who is spiritually minded will not doubt the truth of those seven doctrines listed above. From this fact, it logically follows that one who cannot or will not accept them as true has in reality never been converted.

The evidence, therefore, that the Bible is a message from God to men on this planet is not complete in this book. More can be given. However, what is given should convince any infidel, atheist or doubter that the Bible is a book written by men who were in contact with a Being of unlimited knowledge and power.

Evidence, then, has been given in proof of these facts: There is a supreme Being or God. There is just no way to account for life in all its form and its adaptation to environment apart from God. It has been shown that the complexities of environment and life cannot be accounted for on the ground of chance as taught by evolution. Second, one of the greatest lines of evidence of inspiration of the Bible is prophecy. There is no way to account for the truth of the prophecies concerning the ancient cities and Christ except in one way: The prophets received their knowledge from God. Third, the Bible speaks for itself by giving us facts concerning the physical universe, the spiritual world and the nature of man. These facts were found in the Bible long before they were proven true by science. This is unquestionable evidence of the truth of inspiration. Fourth, consider the testimony of experience. It is a matter of common knowledge that everyone born on this planet, has by sinful conduct, violated the moral law, or is guilty of doing—lying, stealing, and so on—what a Supreme Being has told them not to do. All men, then, who know themselves, are conscious that a tendency toward evil exists deep-rooted in their nature. Every broken home, everyone in prison and every act of evil is the result of yielding to this inward principle of evil. No exercise of will power, no form of education and no restraint can eliminate this evil tendency or principle from the soul. Yet, not only has the character of good moral people been changed for the better, but also those who are guilty of criminal conduct. These changes in character are the result of yielding obedience to certain fundamental principles, such as submission and faith, found only in the Bible. The lives of thousands, then, in all ages have been changed and are being changed for the better, by following instruction found only in the Bible. This is absolute evidence of the truth of inspiration. In view, therefore, of this assembled evidence, it is folly to reject the Bible as the inspired Word of God.